FOOTBALL SUPERSTARS

RONALDO

RULES

SIMON MUGFORD   DAN GREEN

CONTENTS

FOOTBALL SUPERSTARS

RONALDO RULES

Hi, pleased to meet you.

We hope you enjoy our book about Ronaldo!

SIMON

DAN

WELBECK

THIS IS A WELBECK CHILDREN'S BOOK
Published in 2020 by Welbeck Children's Books Limited
An imprint of the Welbeck Publishing Group
20 Mortimer Street, London W1T 3JW
Text, design and illustration © Welbeck Publishing Limited 2020
ISBN: 978 1 78312 533 3

Writer: Simon Mugford
Designer and Illustrator: Dan Green
Design manager: Emily Clarke
Editorial manager: Joff Brown
Production: Nicola Davey

A catalogue record for this book is available from the British Library.

Printed in the UK
10 9 8 7 6 5 4 3 2 1

Statistics and records correct as of October 2019

CHAPTER 1

RONALDO IS THE BEST

RONALDO! RONALDO!

Who is the best footballer in the world? **Ronaldo?** You must be reading this book because you think he is **FANTASTIC, AMAZING** and just **AWESOME** in **every way**, right?

SO WHAT MAKES RONALDO SUCH A GREAT PLAYER?

Speed
One of the fastest players on the pitch.

Dribbling
Famous for running with the ball at his feet.

Tricks
Awesome at back-heels, flicks and super step-overs.

Strength and height
Can easily jump up and head the ball in the net.

GOALS!
Ronaldo scores **LOADS** ... and **LOADS** ... and **LOADS** of them!

8

He is also **BRILLIANT** at free-kicks, taking penalties, creating space . . . **EVERYTHING!**

RONALDO IS THIS GOOD

JUST LOOK AT THE NUMBERS . . .

5 . . . times winner of the Ballon d'Or

More than

700 goals (and he's still scoring!)

6 . . . league titles won in England, Spain and Italy

34

1 **2** **3**

... hat-tricks scored in La Liga

185 MILLION

... Instagram followers

450

... goals scored for Real Madrid

£84 MILLION

... transfer fee from Manchester United to Real Madrid

AND OF COURSE...

that famous shirt number.

7

RONALDO I.D.

NAME:
Cristiano Ronaldo dos Santos Aveiro

NICKNAME:
CR7

DATE OF BIRTH:
5 February 1985

PLACE OF BIRTH: *Funchal in Madeira (Portugal)*

HEIGHT: *1.85 m*

POSITION: *Forward/Left winger*

CLUBS: *Sporting Lisbon, Manchester United, Real Madrid, Juventus*

NATIONAL TEAM: *Portugal*

LEFT OR RIGHT-FOOTED: *Both*

CHAPTER 2

THE BOY WONDER

Ronaldo was born in 1985, on a beautiful, sunny island in the **Atlantic Ocean** called **Madeira.** Ronaldo grew up there with his mum and dad, brother and two sisters.

MADEIRA

His family did not have much money, but they **LOVED** each other very much.

And there was one thing that the whole family **REALLY** loved . . .

FOOTBALL!

Little Cristiano would play *FOOTBALL* any time that he could, usually in the street with his friends.

Sometimes they had to use a **plastic bottle** instead of a **ball!**

If a boy did bring a ball, that boy was in charge of the game. So when Ronaldo finally got a ball, he **always brought it.** He told everyone **how to play** and got very upset if they did not listen. The other boys got upset with Ronaldo, but what could they do? **He was much, much better** than them.

Ronaldo learned to be **fast** and amazed everyone with his **TRICKS** and **TURNS!**

Ronaldo was the **BEST** player in town. Everyone wanted him on their team, even boys who were older and bigger than he was.

WHAT'S IN A NAME?

Ronaldo's full name is

Cristiano Ronaldo dos Santos Aveiro.

His mum named him
Ronaldo after the
former American
president and
Hollywood actor,

RONALD REAGAN.

Love Ron

Why is he
known as
'Ronaldo'?

Because *Cristiano
Ronaldo dos Santos
Aveiro* doesn't fit
on a shirt!

CHAPTER 3

A SPORTING LIFE

As a boy, Ronaldo played for his local teams **Andorinha** and **Nacional.** He was easily the best player, but sometimes his team-mates got upset if Ronaldo didn't pass the ball.

He always wanted to  **WIN** and he always wanted to **SCORE!**

When he was just **12**, Ronaldo made the first big transfer of his life. He was going to play for **Sporting Lisbon,** one of the biggest teams in Portugal.

Lisbon was a long way from home and Ronaldo found it hard living in a big city. He missed his *MUM AND DAD.*

But he knew that as long as he played football, he would be okay. **AND HE WAS!**

Ronaldo scored his **first** ever **professional goal** for Sporting Lisbon when he was **17.**

THIS WAS JUST THE START . . .

Later, when Ronaldo was a **BIG STAR**
at Manchester United, they played against
Sporting Lisbon in the Champions League.

It was **1-1** and United won a free-kick in the
very last minute of the game . . .

Ronaldo stepped up to take the kick.
It was a long way out, but . . . WOW!

The ball flew into the net.

GOoOoOO

He had scored one of his best goals — and it was against his old club.

Ronaldo played for **Sporting Lisbon's**

UNDER-16s

UNDER-17s

UNDER-18s

THE B TEAM

AND

THE FIRST TEAM

ALL IN ONE SEASON.

No other player has ever done that.

He scored a total of five goals for Sporting and won the **Portuguese Super Cup.**

CHAPTER 4

KING RONALDO

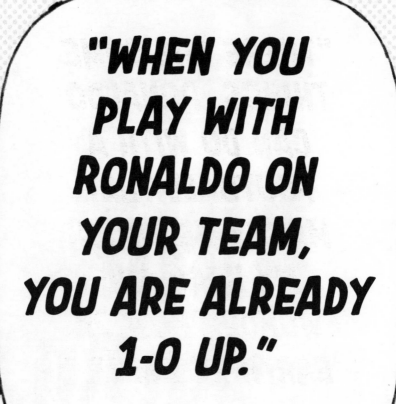

"WHEN YOU PLAY WITH RONALDO ON YOUR TEAM, YOU ARE ALREADY 1-0 UP."

Legendary French footballer and manager, Zinedine Zidane

28

"THERE ARE SOME THINGS RONALDO CAN DO WITH A FOOTBALL THAT MAKES ME TOUCH MY HEAD AND WONDER HOW ON EARTH HE DID IT."

Portuguese football legend, Luis Figo

Scoring a goal with a backheel is a very clever, **cheeky** move. And of course, ***Ronaldo loves backheel goals.***

He scored one against **Rayo Vallecano** in 2012 when he was actually *running away* from the goal.

UNBELIEVABLE!

And he scored a **WONDERFUL** backheel volley against Valencia in 2014.

Ronaldo scores lots of goals, which means lots of **CELEBRATIONS...**

RONALDO'S MOST FAMOUS
CELEBRATION

is when he jumps, turns and lands, arms spread

out with his back to the crowd and shouts:

Siiiiiiiiiii

("YESSSSSSSSS")

RONALDO
7

CHAPTER 5

RONALDO THE MAN ... UNITED

Ronaldo only played for one season in the first team at Sporting Lisbon.

In the summer break, the team played a **friendly** match in their new stadium. It was against one of the biggest clubs in the world,

MANCHESTER UNITED..

Sporting won the game 3-1 and Ronaldo was *BRILLIANT.* The top United players like **Ryan Giggs, Paul Scholes, Rio Ferdinand** and their manager **Sir Alex Ferguson**

were amazed.

WOW!

Ronaldo had signed before United left

to go back to England. Now he was a

Manchester United player.

Manchester United had signed Ronaldo for **12 and a quarter million pounds.** At that time, in 2003, it was the most money that any English team had paid for a teenage player. Cristiano Ronaldo was just **18 years old.**

Sir Alex knew that Ronaldo was going to be a very special player for United, so he gave him the **NUMBER 7** shirt to wear.

This was the number that the United legends **David Beckham, George Best** and **Eric Cantona** had worn. Ronaldo would have to be very special indeed.

SOME OF THE TROPHIES, MEDALS AND AWARDS *RONALDO* WON WHEN HE WAS AT *UNITED.*

PREMIER LEAGUE
2006-07
2007-08
2008-09

FA CUP
2003-04

LEAGUE CUP
2005-06
2008-09

COMMUNITY SHIELD
2007

CHAMPIONS LEAGUE
2007-08

CLUB WORLD CUP
2008

In April 2009, Manchester United were in Portugal, playing **Porto** away in the **Champions League** quarter-final. United needed to win or they would be **OUT** of the competition.

Just **SIX MINUTES** into the game, Ronaldo picked up a pass from **40 yards** out and then took a shot!

GOAAALLL!!

The Porto keeper had no chance!

Ronaldo said it was the **BEST GOAL** he'd ever scored.

The Manchester United fans voted it the

GOAL OF THE DECADE..

CHAPTER 6

THE FAME GAME

Ronaldo is not **just** one of the best known **FOOTBALLERS** in the world. He is one of the most *FAMOUS PEOPLE* on the **planet.**

Over **120 MILLION** fans follow his Facebook page - more than any other footballer.

GRRR!

Kim Kardashian

On Instagram, Ronaldo is the **most** followed person in **the world,** with over **180 MILLION** followers.

The American sports channel **ESPN** named Ronaldo as the world's most famous sportsperson in **2016, 2017, 2018** and **2019.**

In a children's short story competition run by the BBC in 2019, **Ronaldo** was the **real person** that children chose to write about the most.

Back in his home on **Madeira,** people love Ronaldo so much, they named the airport after him!

When the airport opened, a **SCULPTURE** of Ronaldo's head was made to put on display there - **except that it didn't look much like Ronaldo!**

LOTS OF PEOPLE THOUGHT IT WAS FUNNY.

Ronaldo was very *COOL* and **polite.**

He didn't say anything about it.

The funny sculpture has now been replaced with one that looks more like him!

If you are in Madeira, you can even visit a Ronaldo museum! The **MUSEU CR7** displays all of the trophies that Ronaldo has won. **You could be looking around for a long time!**

You could also stay the night at the **CR7 HOTEL** next door.

WELCOME TO MY HOTEL.

ER, HI!

CHECK-IN

And have your photograph taken next to the

RONALDO STATUE.

All these places are easy to find as **the address is:**

In 2015, Ronaldo was named the

WORLD'S MOST CHARITABLE SPORTS STAR.

He has donated lots of money to charities that help **hospitals, children** and **rainforests**.

THANKS, RONALDO!

54

CHAPTER 7

THE GOAL MACHINE

Ronaldo was an amazing player for **United.** He scored *LOADS OF GOALS* and set up lots more for his team-mates.

He scored his ***FIRST GOAL*** for Manchester United in November 2003, against Portsmouth in the Premier League.

UNITED WON 3-0.

His *LAST GOAL* for United was scored against local rivals **Manchester City** at Old Trafford in May 2009.

> ***Some might say*** that was a good goal.

Noel Gallagher, *Manchester City fan*

RONALDO'S MANCHESTER UNITED GOAL RECORD

SEASON	APPEARANCES	GOALS
2003-04	40	6
2004-05	50	9
2005-06	47	12
2006-07	53	23
2007-08	49	42
2008-09	53	26
TOTAL	292	118

Ronaldo has scored **54 hat-tricks** for club and country. *HE'S THE HAT-TRICK KING!*

In nine seasons at **Real Madrid,** he scored a total of **34** hat-tricks in **La Liga.** Nobody has scored more La Liga hat-tricks than **Ronaldo.**

Lionel Messi has *scored 33.*

Ronaldo has also scored **8** *CHAMPIONS LEAGUE* hat-tricks.

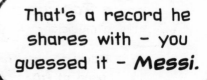

That's a record he shares with – you guessed it – *Messi.*

Portugal's number **7** has scored **8** hat-tricks for his country.

Ronaldo loves scoring hat-tricks in **BIG** games. His three against Switzerland took Portugal to the **2019 Nations League Final.** He also scored **FOUR** against Lithuania in a **EURO 2020** qualifier.

Why is **Ronaldo** like a magician?

Because they are both good at **hat-tricks!**

Some of **Ronaldo's** most *AMAZING GOALS* come from free-kicks.

The **knuckleball** is a very **powerful free-kick** sent directly to the goal.

BOOM!

When Ronaldo, lines up to take a free-kick, he likes to stand with his legs slightly apart, arms hanging by his side.

IT LOOKS EXTRA COOL AND DRAMATIC.

RONALDO WONDER GOAL #2

In Ronaldo's last season for **REAL MADRID**, he scored twice when they played **JUVENTUS** in a **CHAMPIONS LEAGUE** quarter-final.

WOW!

Ronaldo's second goal was an **incredible,** overhead **BICYCLE KICK.**

It was such a **GOOD GOAL,** that even the **Juventus fans** and players **clapped Ronaldo.**

Ronaldo said it was his

BEST EVER GOAL.

This is what others said:

> "IT'S A PLAYSTATION GOAL . . .
> HE SCORED A GOAL THAT WILL
> GO DOWN IN HISTORY . . ."
>
> *Juventus defender Andrea Barzagli*

> **"ABSOLUTELY
> BREATHTAKING!"**
>
> *England legend Gary Lineker*

> "RONALDO CAN NOW LEAVE EARTH
> AND PLAY WITH MARTIANS.
> HE HAS DONE EVERYTHING HERE."
>
> *Ex-Real Madrid defender Alvaro Arbeloa*

CHAPTER 8

IDEAL FOR REAL

65

PREMIER LEAGUE

FA CUP

CHAMPIONS LEAGUE

At Manchester United, Ronaldo won the **PREMIER LEAGUE** three times, the **FA CUP,** the **LEAGUE CUP** and the **CHAMPIONS LEAGUE.**

Cristiano also won the **BALLON D'OR** in 2008, which meant he was the *BEST PLAYER IN THE WORLD.* But he wanted to win even more.

So in 2009, Ronaldo signed for

REAL MADRID

for a world-record fee of

£84 MILLION

WELCOME TO MADRID

Ronaldo was introduced to **80,000** Real Madrid fans at the **Bernabéu stadium.**

They were going **crazy** for their new star. He was going to join the team of **superstar players** like **Raúl, Kaká** and **Sergio Ramos.**

Raúl, the captain, was Madrid's number **7**,

so **Ronaldo** wore number **9** at first.

But when Raúl left . . .

CR7 WAS BACK.

Ronaldo scored in his **first four games** for Madrid. By the end of his first season he'd scored **33 GOALS**.

He ended **2010-11** with **53 GOALS** and won the **European Golden Shoe.**

In **2011-12**, he scored **60 GOALS** and Madrid won **La Liga.**

AND HE KEPT ON SCORING . . .

RONALDO'S MADRID GOAL RECORD

SEASON	APPEARANCES	GOALS
2009-10	35	33
2010-11	54	53
2011-12	55	60
2012-13	55	55
2013-14	47	51
2014-15	54	61
2015-16	48	51
2016-17	46	42
2017-18	44	44
TOTAL	438	450

THE REAL WINNER

RONALDO'S TOP RECORDS, HONOURS AND AWARDS AT REAL MADRID.

REAL MADRID'S ALL-TIME TOP SCORER

450 goals

MOST LA LIGA HAT-TRICKS

34

LA LIGA TOP SCORER

2010-11
2013-14
2014-15

WORLD SOCCER PLAYER OF THE YEAR

2013, 2014
2016, 2017

BALLON D'OR

2013
2014
2016
2017

COPA DEL REY TOP SCORER

2016
2017

Madrid reached the Champions League Final in **2014**. They were playing their local rivals **Atlético Madrid** in **Lisbon,** where Ronaldo began his career, so it was a *VERY* special match for **Ronaldo.**

Atlético were winning 1-0, until **Sergio Ramos** equalised in injury time. They scored two more goals in extra-time and **Ronaldo scored a penalty** at the very end.

THEY WON 4-1.

Madrid were **EUROPEAN CHAMPIONS** for a *TENTH* time. They called it ...

LA DÉCIMA.

NO TEAM HAD DONE THAT BEFORE.

RONALDO, HIS TEAM-MATES AND THE FANS WENT CRAZY!

RONALDO
IS ONE OF MADRID'S
GREATEST PLAYERS.

SEE HOW HE COMPARES WITH SOME OTHER REAL ICONS:

RONALDO *2009-2018*

438

APPEARANCES

450

GOALS

ALFREDO DI STÉFANO *1953-1964*

396
APPEARANCES

308
GOALS

RAÚL
1994-2010

741
APPEARANCES
323
GOALS

FERENC PUSKÁS *1958-1966*

262
APPEARANCES

242
GOALS

From **2013-2018 Ronaldo** was part of an *amazing trio:*

Karim **B**enzema
Gareth **B**ale
Cristiano Ronaldo

BBC

Their rivals at Barcelona were

Lionel **M**essi
Luis **S**uarez
Neymar

MSN

Ronaldo is one of the best players ever to play in the Champions League.

Probably the best.

THESE ARE THE FIVE CHAMPIONS LEAGUE FINALS RONALDO HAS WON.

21 MAY 2008
LUZHNIKI STADIUM, MOSCOW

Manchester United 1-1 Chelsea
(6-5 on penalties)

24 MAY 2014
ESTÁDIO DA LUZ, LISBON

Real Madrid 4-1 Atlético Madrid
(after extra-time)

28 MAY 2016
SAN SIRO STADIUM, MILAN

Real Madrid 1-1 Atlético Madrid
(5-3 on penalties)

3 JUNE 2017
MILLENNIUM STADIUM, CARDIFF

Juventus 1-4 Real Madrid

26 MAY 2018
OLYMPIC STADIUM, KIEV

Real Madrid 3-1 Liverpool

MOST GOALS SCORED IN ONE SEASON

17 Goals
(2013-14)

TOP SCORER FOR SIX SEASONS IN A ROW

2012–13 *(8 goals)*

2013–14 *(12 goals)*

2014–15 *(17 goals)*

2015–16 *(10 goals)*

2016–17 *(12 goals)*

2017–18 *(15 goals)*

MOST CHAMPIONS LEAGUE HAT-TRICKS

8 hat-tricks

Woah!

Don't forget that Messi, did that too

MAN UTD CHAMPIONS LEAGUE HIGHLIGHTS

10 APRIL 2007
QUARTER-FINAL SECOND LEG

Manchester United 7-1 AS Roma *(8-3)*

Ronaldo scored his first two Champions League goals as United thrashed Roma.

21 MAY 2008
FINAL

Manchester United 1-1 Chelsea
(6-5 on penalties)

Cristiano scored and had a penalty saved. This was his first Champions League win.

5 MAY 2009
SEMI-FINAL SECOND LEG

Arsenal 1-3 Manchester United *(1-4)*

He scored a stunning free-kick and a second goal to help put United in the Final.

Any more highlights?

Well, he does put them in his hair sometimes.

HAT-TRICK HERO

18 APRIL 2017
QUARTER-FINAL SECOND LEG

Real Madrid 4-2 Bayern Munich *(6-3)*

Ronaldo scored a hat-trick. The third goal was his 100th in the Champions League.

2 MAY 2017
SEMI-FINAL FIRST LEG

Real Madrid 3-0 Atlético Madrid

Another game, another hat-trick as Ronaldo demolished Atlético.

12 MAR 2019
LAST-16 SECOND LEG

Juventus 3-0 Atlético Madrid *(3-2)*

Another incredible hat-trick against Atlético.
This time Ronaldo was playing for Juventus.

101 GOALS

Ronaldo scored twice for Madrid against Paris St-Germain in a last-16 match in 2018.

They were his 100th and 101st Champions League goals for Madrid.

Ronaldo was the **FIRST PLAYER** to score **more than 100 Champions League goals** for the same club.

CHAPTER 10

PORTUGAL'S HERO

Ronaldo made his debut for Portugal in **2003** and has been the **captain** since **2008**.

He is easily one of their **BEST EVER PLAYERS.**

Here's why:

ALL-TIME TOP SCORER

93 goals

MOST CAPPED PLAYER

160 caps

MOST HAT-TRICKS SCORED

8

MOST EUROPEAN CHAMPIONSHIP MATCHES PLAYED

21

MOST WORLD CUP FINALS MATCHES PLAYED

17

MOST GOALS SCORED IN EUROPEAN CHAMPIONSHIP FINALS

9

NATIONS LEAGUE WINNER

2019

WORLD CUP 2006

When Portugal played **England** in the **2006 World Cup** quarter-final, Ronaldo was up against some of his team-mates from **Manchester United**.

Wayne Rooney got a red card and it looked like **Ronaldo** had helped get him sent off. Then Ronaldo scored the winning penalty in the shoot-out that **sent England home**.

The England fans were **not happy** with Ronaldo.

REF!

BUT, Ronaldo and Rooney were still friends . . . and they went on to win the **Premier League together!**

SORRY WAYNE!

93

RONALDO'S EUROPEAN CHAMPIONSHIPS

YEAR	PORTUGAL PLACE	GOALS
2004	RUNNERS-UP	2
2008	QUARTER-FINALS	1
2012	SEMI-FINALS	3
2016	CHAMPIONS	3

RONALDO'S WORLD CUPS

YEAR	PORTUGAL PLACE	GOALS
2006	FOURTH PLACE	1
2010	ROUND OF 16	1
2014	GROUP STAGE	1
2018	ROUND OF 16	4

Only four players have ever scored in four World Cups.

CHAMPIONS OF EUROPE

Ronaldo led Portugal to their first major international title in **2016**, when they won the ***EUROPEAN CHAMPIONSHIP***.

During the tournament, he became Portugal's **most capped player** and scored ***THREE*** goals.

In the final against **_FRANCE_**, who were the host nation, he came off **injured** after just 25 minutes. But **Ronaldo shouted** from the sidelines, urging his team-mates to **_VICTORY_**.

He lifted the trophy after their 1–0 win.

In the final, a swarm of moths flew around the stadium!

PORTUGAL ICON

SEE HOW RONALDO MEASURES UP AGAINST THE OTHER PORTUGAL GREATS:

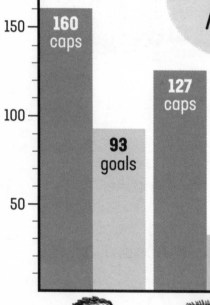

160 caps
93 goals
127 caps
32 goals
64 caps
41 goals

RONALDO
2003-

LUIS FIGO
1991-2006

EUSÉBIO
1961-1963

CHAPTER 11

RONALDO
VS
MESSI

The **argument** about who the **best player** is will go on **FOREVER**.

The Ballon d'Or (The Golden Ball)
is a **PRIZE** awarded to
the **best footballer**
each year.

THESE ARE THE RESULTS SINCE
RONALDO FIRST WON IT.

YEAR	1ST PLACE		2ND PLACE	
2008	RONALDO		MESSI	
2009	MESSI		RONALDO	
2010	MESSI		ANDRÉS INIESTA	
2011	MESSI		RONALDO	

HELLO!

YEAR	1ST PLACE	2ND PLACE
2012	MESSI	RONALDO
2013	RONALDO	MESSI
2014	RONALDO	MESSI
2015	MESSI	RONALDO
2016	RONALDO	MESSI
2017	RONALDO	MESSI
2018	LUKA MODRIĆ	RONALDO

GRRR!

HEAD TO HEAD

 = RONALDO

 = MESSI

CLUB GOALS

 605 **604**

INTERNATIONAL GOALS

 93 **68**

CLUB HAT-TRICKS

 46 **45**

INTERNATIONAL HAT-TRICKS

 8 **6**

CLUB PENALTIES SCORED

103 **70**

INTERNATIONAL PENALTIES SCORED

 9 **14**

CHAMPIONS LEAGUE MEDALS

 5 **4**

CHAMPIONS LEAGUE GOALS

 128 **112**

WORLD CUP GOALS

 7 **6**

LEAGUE TITLES

 6 **10**

CUP TITLES

 12 **17**

GOLDEN SHOE WINS

 4 **6**

RONALDO vs MESSI in LA LIGA

SEASON	RONALDO GOALS	MESSI GOALS
2009-10	26	34
2010-11	40	31
2011-12	46	50
2012-13	34	46
2013-14	31	28
2014-15	48	43
2015-16	35	26
2016-17	25	37
2017-18	26	34
TOTAL	311	329

CHAPTER 12

SUPERHUMAN

KEEPING FIT

by Sid Ups

Ronaldo is famous for being one of the **FITTEST, FASTEST** and **STRONGEST** footballers in the world.

He wasn't always that way.

The skinny teenager at Sporting Lisbon worked *really,* **REALLY** hard to become a **SUPERHUMAN ATHLETE.**

BEFORE

AFTER

SUPERMAN

When he signed for Juventus in 2018, Ronaldo was **33 years old**. But the medical report said that he was as fit as a **20 year-old!**

At the **2018 World Cup,** his running speed was **33.98 KM/H!** *Ronaldo was the fastest player in the tournament.*

STEP OVER STAR

Ronaldo is the **master** of the **step over** - a trick that makes his opponent think he's *going one way . . . but then goes another way.*

HE RUNS HARD, THEN SWINGS ONE FOOT AROUND THE BALL.

THEN SWINGS THE OTHER FOOT, THE SAME WAY VERY FAST!

AND GETS PAST THE DEFENDER!

THE RONALDO CHOP

Ronaldo even has a trick that he invented himself! *Check out The Ronaldo Chop!*

1

HE HOPS OVER THE BALL AND LANDS WITH ONE FOOT IN FRONT OF THE BALL.

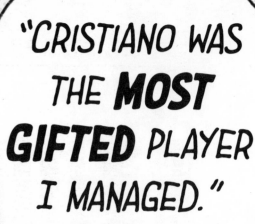

"CRISTIANO WAS THE **MOST GIFTED** PLAYER I MANAGED."

Sir Alex Ferguson

"WHEN RONALDO GETS THE BALL, YOU CAN JUST LEAVE HIM TO IT WHILE HE BEATS PLAYER AFTER PLAYER."

Ryan Giggs

CHAPTER 13

£100 MILLION MAN

In 2018, Italian club Juventus signed Ronaldo for an incredible

£100 MILLION!

It was the ***BIGGEST*** transfer in **ITALY** and it made Ronaldo the **most expensive** player aged ***OVER 30***.

JUVENTUS SEASON #1

APPEARANCES	43
GOALS	28

SERIE A CHAMPIONS
2018-19

SUPERCOPPA ITALIANA
2018

SERIE A MOST VALUABLE PLAYER
2018-19

Ronaldo is the first player to win the league in England, Spain and Italy.

HOW MUCH?!

£100 million is **_A LOT_** of money. But what else could you buy with all that cash?

TWO _Falcon 7x private jets_

100 McLaren P1 supercars

ONE billionaire's superyacht

RONALDO RECORDS
(YOU MIGHT NOT KNOW)

Top FIFA Club World Cup Scorer: *7 goals*

Most international goals in calendar year: *32 goals*

Oldest player to score a hat-trick at a World Cup

First player to score in every minute of a football game

Only player to score more than 50 goals for six seasons in a row

Most UEFA Best Player Awards: *3*

QUIZ TIME!

How much do you know about **Ronaldo?** Try this quiz to find out, then test your friends!

1. How many goals did Ronaldo score for Real Madrid?

----

2. On which island was Ronaldo born?

----

3. Who was his manager at Manchester United?

----

4. What is the name of Ronaldo's first professional club?

----

5. In which year did he win his first Ballon d'Or?

----

6. How many hat-tricks did Ronaldo score in La Liga?

----

7. In which year did Portugal win the European Championship?

----

8. How much did Juventus pay for Ronaldo in 2018?

----

9. Who is Ronaldo's biggest rival in football?

----

10. How many goals did he score in his first season at Juventus?

The answers are on the next page. *But no peeking!*

ANSWERS

1. 450

2. Madeira

3. Sir Alex Ferguson

4. Sporting Lisbon

5. 2008

6. 34

7. 2016

8. £100 million

9. Lionel Messi

10. 28

RONALDO:
WORDS YOU NEED TO KNOW

Ballon d'Or
Award given to the male player who has played the best over a year. Awarded each December by France Football magazine.

Copa Del Rey
Spanish knockout cup competition.

FA Community Shield
Match between winners of the previous season's Premier League and the FA Cup.

FA Cup
English knockout cup competition.

FIFA Club World Cup
Knockout cup competition between clubs from around the world.

La Liga
The top football league in Spain.

Premier League
The top football league in England *(also called the Premiership)*.

Serie A
The top football league in Italy.

UEFA Champions League
European club competition held every year. The winner is the best team in Europe.

UEFA Nations League
Competition for national sides in UEFA. Held every two years.

Supercopa de España
Competition between winners and runners-up of the previous season's La Liga and Copa Del Rey.

Supercoppa Italiana
Match between winners of the previous season's Serie A and the Coppa Italia.

ABOUT THE AUTHORS

Simon's first job was at the Science Museum, making paper aeroplanes and blowing bubbles big enough for your dad to stand in. Since then he's written all sorts of books about the stuff he likes, from dinosaurs and rockets, to llamas, loud music and of course, football. Simon has supported Ipswich Town since they won the FA Cup in 1978 (it's true - look it up) and once sat next to Rio Ferdinand on a train. He lives in Kent with his wife and daughter, two tortoises and a cat.

Dan has drawn silly pictures since he could hold a crayon. Then he grew up and started making books about stuff like trucks, space, people's jobs, *Doctor Who* and *Star Wars*. Dan remembers Ipswich Town winning the FA cup but he didn't watch it because he was too busy making a Viking ship out of brown paper. As a result, he knows more about Vikings than football. Dan lives in Suffolk with his wife, son, daughter and a dog that takes him for very long walks.